"Encouragement, Inspiration, Hope"

30 DAY-DEVOTIONAL

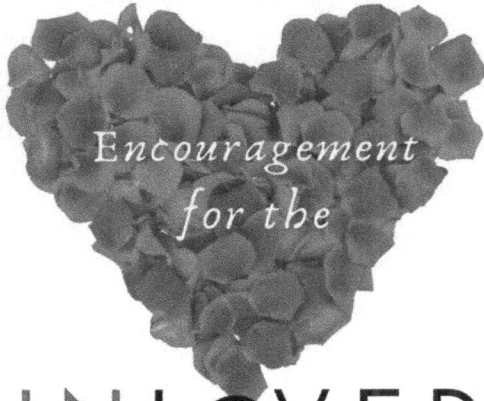

Encouragement
for the

UNL❁VED
WIFE

PRAYER
AFFIRMATION
HEALING

DR. MARITA KINNEY

Attention Reader:

This is Your Book. Feel free to highlight in it, circle words, write, or fold pages. The best reading experience is when you participate and make the words speak into your very own life.

Lord I pray that you pour out your love unto every marriage represented through these pages. Heal the brokenhearted, soften the cold hearts, and restore the woman reading this book in Jesus Name, Amen.

Table of Contents

———— ·❀· ————

MARITAKinney

INTRODUCTION

Enjoy

Introduction

If you're reading this book, chances are you either feel un-loved by your spouse at this very moment, or at some point in time, you have identified as feeling unloved by your spouse or under-appreciated. I wanted to take a moment to write a book that spoke to the brokenhearted, feeling alone, unappreciated, unloved, insecure, not protected and very vulnerable woman at this time in your marriage.

It's very important that you realize that in order to become the woman that you would like to become, you have to get to a safe place where you're healthy in your mind, body and spirit. Chances are that you gave your power away and didn't realize it. If you depend on someone to make you happy, then you also have given them the ability to make you unhappy. Often when we feel broken in our spirit, it affects how we operate in our daily life. It affects how you love those around you. It could be your children, your husband, your parents, your friends, your coworkers, whoever. Let's be honest, when you don't feel good, we're not performing at 100% and whenever you're not performing at your best, it will show up in other areas of your life.

This book is intended to give you the support that you need at this moment. Most women who are feeling unloved in their marriage are suffering in silence. Most women are not going around letting everyone know how hard they are battling inside by announcing to the world, "Hello, I feel unloved, my husband is making me feel like crap right now." No one is advertising it. Secondly, no one has the power to make you feel unloved or like crap. It's simply the choice that you make in response to something that was done or said. Please don't be surprised by the statements that I make in this book. There will be times throughout this book that I'll remind you that you always have a choice. It's true, you choose to *feel unloved and like crap*. You also have the power to reject such negativity if it were done or said to you. The woman reading this book, may be reading it discreetly, looking for some sort of healing so that you can deal with the life that you have *chosen*. Yes, I said chosen. You have to take some responsibility in the situation, even if it's admitting to the fact that you said "I Do" to the man that once made you feel loved enough to marry him. Let that sink in because that can be a hard pill to swallow. Another hard pill to swallow is the reality of knowing that there is nothing wrong with you.

I want to give you some advice that has helped me through the course of my life where I have felt very similar to you. I had to take some responsibility for my outcome as well. Often, we underestimate the value or the power within us, and that power allows us to change and create. You have the power to manifest change in your life. It's true! I remember reading a book by

Marianne Williamson called *"Return to Love"*, and one of the things that I remember reading in that book was that we have more power than we realize. I remember Marianne stating that, "anything other than love is not true."

I had to really reflect on that statement because it really spoke to me. So then I thought to myself, *the way that I'm feeling, isn't true?* And whenever things are not true, they're not of God, because God is truth and God is love. Therefore anything outside of love is not true and it's indeed a lie. I had to realize that I had the power to change some things within my marriage, and I didn't want to play the victim anymore. The issue wasn't my husband, the issue was me. That was my hard pill for me to swallow. I was self- sabotaging my marriage because of what I decided to focus my attention on. If you want to see good in your marriage, it's there. The same is true if you'd like to find something to upset you. Either decision is true.

In fact, whatever you focus on will magnify. So this book is intended to shift your focus so that the right things in your life can be magnified. By refocusing, you can experience a loving relationship with your husband that's beautiful. You have the power to shift your mindset and how you view your marriage, your life, your children, your spouse, everything that's important to you. You have the power to enjoy it if you choose to. So I'm going to ask you before we go onto chapter one, what are you paying attention to?

Please take a moment to answer these questions within your heart. You can write them down or answer then silently within. This book really isn't about your husband, it's about you. Please take a moment and truthfully find out where you are as a wife.

Questionnaire:

1. Do you hold your husband's hand?

2. Do you speak highly of him to others?

3. Are you a good lover?

4. Have you ignored him by staying on your phone?

5. Have you prioritized your kids and not your marriage?

6. Are you a wife of integrity?

7. Have you encouraged your husband in the last 30 days?

8. Do you consult with your husband on the finances?

9. Do you passionately kiss your husband? (Not a peck like you kiss your children.)

10. Do you dress up for your husband like you did for a first date?

11. Do you pray with your husband?

12. Do you encourage his dreams?

13. Do you plan your life with him?

14. Have you flirted with your husband lately?

15. Have you undermined his authority as head of the house?

16. Are you slow to anger?

17. Have you gone out your way to show your love for him lately?

18. Do you publically knowledge him?

19. Do you compare him to other men?

20. Have you asked him about his goals or vision?

21. Do you laugh with him?

22. Do you desire to please him and honor him?

23. Are you loving or loveable?

24. Is his heart safe with you?

25. Are his secrets safe with you?

26. Are you submissive or dominant over him?

01

CHAPTER

01

The Gap

———————— ❧ ————————

This is a really interesting chapter because there's a gap that currently exists in your world and this is the gap between where you are and where you desire to be emotionally within your marriage. Right now, you may desire love, affection, and some other things from your spouse or maybe other areas of your life too, but for the sake of this book, we're talking specifically about your marriage.

There's a gap that says you're missing something, there's something that's going lacking and you're not feeling fulfilled. In fact, you're feeling unloved. I want to first remind you that you are loved, you are beautiful, you are appreciated, you are worthy, you are respected, and you're a great woman. You have the ability to close the gap in your marriage, and I'm going to share the secret with you and how to do so.

Often times, we give our power away to our husbands, we just do. I don't know why, but sometimes as women we are looking for people to validate us, to pat us on the back and say, "You're beautiful." We're looking for people to stroke our ego, especially our husbands. Who doesn't want to feel loved, adored and admired by their significant other? Of course, we're women, we desire that. The problem is when we don't get it, we think something's wrong. I want to encourage you to discover what the gap in your marriage truly looks like. How big of a gap is it?

We give that responsibility to our spouse and expect for them to fill in that gap within us. You're probably thinking, what in the world is she talking about? I'm talking about your relationship with God. Yes, your relationship with God has everything to do with the empty holes in your life that you're searching for someone or something else to fill or should I say fulfill. The danger in that is you're placing your happiness at the mercy of someone else and that's very dangerous because if someone has the power to make you happy, that means you have also given them the power to make you unhappy. I also mentioned this earlier in this book because I want you to understand that it's your responsibility to choose happiness in your life. Yu have to first decide that you want it. As women we are guilty of punishing ourselves by what we attract, accept, create, and self-afflict.

You have to take your power back connecting to God. Truly the closer you get to God, the smaller the gap becomes where you don't look for other people to fulfill that need. When you have a strong relationship with God, it gives you a certain level of confidence, it gives you identity, it gives you purpose. No one can take your joy, no one can make you feel unloved because simply, you know that's not true. You are a daughter of the King of Kings. Of course, you're loved, of course you're valuable, of course you're worthy. Do you know who you are? Do you know whose you are?

Once you discover whose you are, the gap will begin to close where no one or nothing can make you feel insignificant. No one can make you feel unloved not even your husband because you walk with confidence knowing that you're loved in spite of, what's going on around you. One of the interesting things about "the gap," is that we can oftentimes compare our relationship with other people and that can also magnify whatever you're lacking or whatever you're desiring at the moment. The best way to get love is to give love. As wives we must stop looking at what the husbands are doing or not doing, and began to look within. You cannot control other people; however, you are responsible for how you react. As you continue to read this book, I challenge you to look at what type of wife you are and shift the focus off of your husband. You have the power within you to love and receive love. You are a lovable person and you deserve to feel love. You can begin to feel loved by first feeling the love from God. God loves you and your happiness matters to him. But above all, God wants you to have joy. Joy is different from happiness. Happiness comes in spirts and from temporary moments of satisfaction. Joy comes from God and remains permeant in your spirit. It won't change with circumstance, like happiness does. What God gives to us, no one can take away.

"The heart of her husband trusts in her, and he will have no lack of gain. She does him good, and not harm, all the days of her life." Proverbs 31:11-12

Day 1

Affirmation:

I will not say anything negative to my husband or about my husband. I will affirm and encourage him daily. I have the divine power within me to shift the atmosphere of my home into a loving environment of peace and refuge. I am loved and I give unconditional love to my husband, And So It Is.

Prayer

Lord I ask that you soften my heart to see the good in my husband and to love him without conditions. I ask that you remove all negative thoughts about him from my mind and replace them with gratitude and appreciation.

Day 2

Affirmation:

I give and receive love easily and unconditionally. I trust God to give me strength and divine wisdom to communicate my love to my husband and others. I am loveable. I am worthy of love, respect, and honor. Because I love, honor and respect myself. I know that I am made wonderfully in the image of God. I am loved, And So It Is.

Day 3

Affirmation

I will speak to my husband with a pleasant soft tone so that he can hear my heart. He hears my femininity when I speak to him. I communicate with love and not fear. I exercise self-control and do not belittle him. I build him up and honor him. I love him and I am Loved, And So It Is.

Prayer

Lord help me to choose my words wisely. I do not want to be a foolish woman with an uncontrollable mouth. If I cannot find the words to say out of love, please arrest my tongue and don't allow me to say anything. I desire to be a loving person, fill my heart with your love and allow it to overflow to my marriage. Turn my husband's hurt towards me and not allow it to harden or grow cold. Through you all things are possible and I yield my marriage to you Lord. I trust you, Amen. And So, It Is!

Day 4

Affirmation:

I will honor my husband with my words and my thoughts. I will not speak badly of him to anyone. I recognize that when I speak ill of my husband, I speak ill of myself because we are one. Through divine power I shall seek only the truth and the truth shall flow from my heart. That truth is love and anything outside of love is a lie that I will no longer accept. And So It Is.

Prayer:

God almighty I confess that I can do things better in my marriage. Instead of looking for solutions outside of my marriage, I know to look inward and pray to you Lord. Give me the courage to trust you and to bring hope into my heart. I ask for Your forgiveness Lord for any negative thing that I have spoken about my husband or have held in my heart. Remind me to speak praises and kind words of him that lifts him up. I offer grace for his shortcoming and not conviction. Amen, And So It Is!

02

CHAPTER

02

Comparing

———⟿———

We live in a day and age where a lot of people post their highlights on social media and what that tends to do is highlight that person's life but it can also magnify the gaps in yours. As you learn in chapter one there are gaps that exist and they exist because there's a lack between our relationship with God where we want to be and where we are, and that gap leaves a lot of room for insecurities, a lot of room for us to compare our lives to other people.

And you simply want to work hard at your relationship with God to close the gap, to not leave room for manipulation from other people or outside influences. So when you compare your life to other people, you must realize it's a lie. And the reason why it's a lie is because I was always taught that half-truth is a whole lie. And most people on social media, most people in your church or your day to day life, whoever it is, most people are only showing you one side of the story which is their success story. Not many people are sharing their failures with you.

And so if you're only showing someone half the story, you're presenting them a whole lot because the truth of the matter is you're not always happy, every day is not a vacation, every day you're not smiling and taking selfies and showing the world how great your life is. There are some days where you wake up and you're sad or the person may just not be on point that day as far as how they look. So they're not going to present themselves to the world with their hair undone or whatever the case is, they're only going to show you what they want you to see. And so you start to see the highlight of everyone's life and then you start to magnify, "Oh, the shortcomings of your husband."

You have to ask yourself, "Is that fair?" Because there are some ups and downs in everyone's marriage but the world is not privileged to see the not so good stuff in your marriage because you're married, it's private, there are certain things that you and your spouse will go through that are simply just between the two of you, it's no one's business. Every argument is not to be had in front of the world or even your children, your family or your friends. Some conversations which I think all your conversations dealing with hot topics should be between the two.

And when you start to compare with a social media or with a romance novel, you're comparing your marriage to a fantasy. That's what's going on and whenever you compare your mirrors to a fantasy it's just like a husband comparing his wife to a porn star. Now, I know that may sound very harsh and I'm sorry to be so vulgar, but whoever the porn star is, you don't see her picking up her kids from school, you don't see her paying her bills, you don't see her cooking dinner, you don't see her shopping, you don't see her doing anything but having sex with someone. And so when men look at those visuals simulations all day long, they have a fantasy in their head and then they hold their wife into an unexpected expectation. Not saying that all men do this, I'm just using that as an example so that you can see how on both sides there could be fantasies that are lived out in your mind, things that you're desiring and wanting and you're expecting that into your real life not realizing, "Hey, I'm bringing a fantasy and trying to make it realistic for me."

So try not to ever compare your marriage with anyone because if someone tells you that they're always happy, 365 days a year, they're lying, they're lying. The word of God tells us that if you get married that you're going to have trouble. So if that's the case, how can every day be rosy?

So always remember, never to compare yourself to others. Your story can be just as beautiful as anyone else is. The moments that you share between you and your husband are between two, you may decide to share some things, and you may decide to share vulnerable moments if that's okay with you and your husband and hopes of helping someone else not live in a fantasy.

So, what's the identity of your marriage? What makes your marriage special? Because as mentioned, what you focus on, what we magnify, so I'm challenging you to get a journal and begin to write down all of the things that you find special in your marriage, depending on how long you've been married, you may be feeling like your bad times are outweighing the good times. You may feel that way and that even may be true in some cases, but if you search hard enough, you'll begin to see that there's some good there. And when you see the good start to reminisce on how that made you feel, because I want you to shift your energy into what you don't like versus what you do like about your spouse.

As you begin to think of all the things that you enjoy about your spouse, that's what you'll begin to focus on and your energy will shift towards your marriage and even towards your spouse, and they'll be able to feel. Trust me, your husband knows that you're feeling unloved right now. Your husband knows that you don't like him very much right now. They know, they know. So as we move along in this book, I hope that you get the tools that you need at least to look at things differently from your perspective. No one wants to be a negative Nancy. So the purpose of this book is to get you to change your perspective. When you take something to the altar, you're not asking God to change it, but the miracle is when he changes your perspective of it. So taking something to the altar is altering how you look at it.

Are you constantly comparing your marriage to how it used to be? Well I have good news and bad news for you. I'll start with the bad news: Those days are gone. It's the past and it no longer exists. If you decide to live in the past, I'm afraid to say this to you but your marriage is dead. Nothing in the past is real, it's all gone away. The only thing that is real, is the present moment.

The good news is: You can begin today to create the marriage that you desire. First you must look at the root of any issue that making you feel unloved.

Stress comes with marriage. Not to mention children, bills, and lack of intimacy add fuel to the fire. That's right ladies, if your husband is being unloving towards you it could be that he is stress in one of the following areas:

- Lack of Sex
- Lack of Sleep
- Working Long hours
- Not fulfilling his dreams
- Feeling unsupported
- Finances are unstable
- Health Issues
- Feeling Disrespected by you, family, or children
- Body changes

Go through the list and pray about what could be contributing to the feeling that you may have at times. Believe it or not, if you have not been making love to your king on the regular then he may be in need of some sexual healing. I know it can be challenging to become intimate when you need more love, but let's face it. If you're holding out, then your just as guilty to contributing to the stress of your marriage. Besides, where else is he supposed to go and get "some" from? If your man is walking around angry, consider how often your making love to him. Sadly, often times other women and men can also sense a sexual deprived person. Do not leave any room for temptation. Don't let your husband leave home hungry. Did you know that men feel rejected when woman are too tired for sex, don't feel good, or not in the mood? I had no idea. I read several books and articles sharing this fact. My husband and I even wrote a book about it titled, "Not Tonight, I'm Tired". Woman loved that book and men were glad to see a book out on the market that spoke for them. That leads me to my next example of stress in the marriage.

Lack of sleep- Your husband could be running on "E". It's his energy is low and he feels empty and sluggish, it's hard to be in a good mode. Try to allow him to rest and lighten his load when you can. Even a glass of water feels heavy if you hold it for days at a time. Pray and ask God how you can be more of a helpmate to him.

Those are just some examples to show you how daily stress can indeed affect your marriage. Ego wants everything to be about you. However, I challenge you to also think about your husband. As women we cannot always control things or what happens, but we do have a choice in how we respond. I always ask myself this question when I think I'm about to trip, "Marita whatever your about to say or do, is it going to bring peace and honor God?" If the answer is *No* to either question, I know not to act or respond in the way that I was considering.

Lastly, keep your friends in mind, well not really. When it comes to your marriage, your friends have no say so and their opinions should not be considered. I say that because people tend to give advice that they wouldn't take. It's true. Although your friends may mean well, sometimes their advice is bias, not mature, self-led instead of spirit led, and you must always consider the source. I'm sure that you have some wise friends, but unless God is speaking through them, I would not trust their advice, even if they mean well. Once you make a convent with God, you should get your guidance from him.

Be care not to find yourself envying your single friends. There are pros and cons to everyone's life and it's your job to make the most out of the life that you have chosen. The saying, "The grass is not always greener on the other side" is not just for comparing relationship, but it also refers to anything in your life that you are trying to compare. Everything in life has its season, accept your season and be grateful.

"Through Love Serve One Another."- *Galatians 5:13*

Day 5

Affirmation:

I will seek God daily for guidance and wisdom in every area of my life. When I am whole, I can love without restrictions. I choose to have joy no matter what the circumstances are. I choose to be kind, loving, and uplifting. I will not complain about anything, I will see the beauty in everything. And It Is So.

Prayer:

Lord I thank you for blessing me with my amazing husband. Put a spirit of love and acceptance in me towards my husband. I don't want to change him, but accept who you have created him to be. I am imperfect and I married an imperfect man. Teach me how to operate as one. Forgive me for judging him. Amen, And So It Is!

Day 6

Affirmation:

I will encourage my husband and listen to his heart. I will be slow to anger and offense. I will have a positive attitude and greet him with joy. I love to see him smile and I choose to smile because I am loved and have joy in my heart. My husband can always count on me for a smile. And It Is So.

Prayer:

Lord help me to hold my peace. I ask that you help me with self-control and temperance. Becoming easily frustrated does not allow me to become my best-self. I desire to display love in all things. Search my heart Lord and remove anything that is not like you. Fill me up with love, patience, joy, peace, kindness, goodness, gentleness, self-control, and faithfulness. Amen, And So It Is!

Day 7

Affirmation:

I AM Loved. I give and receive unconditional love easily and effortlessly.

Prayer:

Who shall separate us from the love of Christ? Shall tribulation, or distress, or persecution, or famine, or nakedness, or danger, or sword? As it is written, "For your sake we are being killed all the day long; we are regarded as sheep to be slaughtered." No, in all these things we are more than conquerors through him who loved us. For I am sure that neither death nor life, nor angels nor rulers, nor things present nor things to come, nor powers, nor height nor depth, nor anything else in all creation, will be able to separate us from the love of God in Christ Jesus our Lord. So, we have come to know and to believe the love that God has for us. God is love, and whoever abides in love abides in God, and God abides in him. What then shall we say to these things? If God is for us, who can be against us? Trust in him at all times, O people; pour out your heart before him; God is a refuge for us. Selah Trust in him at all times, O people; pour out your heart before him; God is a refuge for us. Selah. And So, It Is!

Day 8

Affirmation:

I AM Understood and God Heals My Heart and Knows My Pain.

Prayer:

Thank You Lord,

*You keep track of all my sorrows. You have collected all **my tears** in your bottle. You have recorded each one in your book. There is no fear in love, but perfect love casts out fear. For fear has to do with punishment, and whoever fears has not been perfected in love. For I know the plans I have for you, declares the* LORD*, plans for welfare and not for evil, to give you a future and a hope. For the mountains may depart and the hills be removed, but my steadfast love shall not depart from you, and my covenant of peace shall not be removed," says the* LORD*, who has compassion on you. And So, It Is!*

03

CHAPTER

03

The Wait

———— ·※· ————

How many times do we get anxious when we're told to wait? I know sometimes I do because we want God to do something in our lives right now, we want to see everything happen right now. And having patients, when you're not feeling good in your spirit can seem like eternity. So what's the purpose of waiting? Well, I want you to number one, do the things that I've already mentioned in this book, which are to close the gap. Number two, to not compare yourself to others. And number three, write down the good things about your marriage or the things that have happened in the past that made you smile.

The purpose of this is to shift your perspective of your marriage, we don't want to talk about now, we want to talk about the history. Remember meeting your spouse and how you fell. Think about when you fell in love, think about when you're at the altar and you exchange your vows and you wanted to spend the rest of your life with this person. Because we go through seasons and we change and we have to rely on each other to just stay with us even during our hard times, and your spouse

very well could be going through a tough time that you're una-
ware of.

Do not try to fix your husband. While you wait on God to
repair things, continue to work on yourself.

So I want you to shift your energy off of your husband and I
want you to focus on you, because you need to be the best version of you no matter what. The best version of you should not
be contingent on how you feel in your marriage. I know this is
going to be difficult, but I need you to do this for you.

As wives, as mothers, we tend to put ourselves on the back
burner a lot, and when you let yourself go and when you
stopped taking care of you, it makes it very difficult for other
people to want to be around you. If you're negative, if you're
letting yourself go, if you're not loving yourself, it makes it difficult for other people to love you too.

One of my favorite sayings is you teach people how to treat
you, so if you're not doing a very good job at loving yourself,
chances are you have taught other people how to treat you and
they can become or seeing unloving. But like I said, this book
really isn't about your spouse, this book really is about the unloved you. Now, you're probably reading this book and you're
probably saying to yourself, "Marita, but you don't understand
my husband is doing this or my husband is doing that," and I
totally get it but at the end of the day, you have an obligation
to love you, you have an obligation to become the best version
of you and to ray your mental standard for yourself so high that

no one can take away, how you feel about yourself? Because it goes back to the gap and getting closer to God.

And as you begin to work on your relationship with God, the gap will close. You'll start to feel good about yourself and other people around you will notice the change in the shift within. So if you're looking for a miracle in your marriage, I encourage you to work on you. So while you're waiting for God to change something in your marriage, don't get discouraged and think that waiting means that you're doing nothing. No, you're working on you and you're waiting on different results to happen in your marriage, different outcomes.

But through prayer, God was showing me that when you are working, you are putting a lot of pressure on yourself. I'm trying this and it won't work, I'm trying that and it won't work. No, so work on you. Don't work on your marriage right now, work on you and allow God to do the work. So while you're waiting, he's a working, you have to trust God in all things. God is the most beautiful, powerful, omnipresent spirit that exists. And you can't limit God thinking that he can't do something as simple as fiction marriage.

God is so big, you have to trust him. So allow God to work on your marriage while you're waiting on God to do that work on you. So what are some things that you can do to work on yourself? Could it be your self-image? Could it be a regimen? You wake up every day and you'd tell yourself you're beautiful. I actually wake up every day and I hug myself and I say, "Good morning," that's something that I learned to do good morning,

Day 13

Affirmation:

I will not be distracted by lust. I am a strong woman of integrity and I do not respond to toxic ideas or imaginations. I have the power of the Lord within me to overcome my ego. My true self is rooted in the Lord and I am made in the imagine of God and my identity shall reflect who I am. And So It Is!

Prayer:

God your grace is sufficient. You have loved me when I didn't love myself and I thank you for your faithfulness. Teach me to love myself and my spouse the way that you love me. I can do all things through Christ and I believe that unconditional love is possible within my marriage. Lord heal the wounds that my husband carries and make his burden light. Although, I don't know what he's going through, I do understand that the absence of love is fear and hurt. Counsel him Lord and guide him to his healing. Amen. And So It Is.

04

CHAPTER

04

Decide to Love Yourself

———————✦———————

When you decide to love yourself, other people will love you too. Chances are, you may feel unloved because you're not doing a great job of loving yourself. Now, of course, your children, your spouse, your friends and whoever are supposed to love you, but when you love yourself, you remind other people why they love you too. When you make a decision to love yourself in this season of feeling unloved, remind yourself why you love you. I remember my grandmother used to tell me, "Marita it's your job to like you. If you don't love or like yourself others won't either." That saying never left my spirit. It's true. We like to blame others for how we decide to feel because it supports the story that we tell ourselves. In reality, we change that story by choosing to give love and to feel it. Deciding to love yourself and others is a choice. You cannot put conditions on how you love someone based on how they treat you. Then expect them to love you unconditionally. That's a bit unfair, wouldn't you say? That's sending a message that you want someone to do something that you're not willing to do yourself. If you want unconditional, you must give it.

You can decide to change your life at any given moment. And if you're not sure how to do that, then go back to chapter one and spend some more time with God. Is it that simple? Yes, it is. Changing your life is so simple as changing your mind, interrupting your bad habits, your bad conversations, your bad self-esteem. It's literally a change in perspective that you see yourself. When you decide to love yourself, you'll become easier to love and people enjoy being around you.

Normally, when someone doesn't love their self, they are not really fun to be around. Typically, the signs of someone who didn't love their selves are they're mean, insecure, bashful, indecisive, bitter, angry, violent, abusive, uncaring, unloving, defensive, victimize, boring. Those are some of the signs of someone who's unhappy because if you hurt, you hurt other people. If you're feeling unloved, you're more than likely are going to say unloving things or give off the energy that tells people, "I don't feel loved and the reality is no one enjoys being around someone who's glooming me." It's exhausting and it's draining.

You could be around them for a little bit but you don't want to be the person who's an energy sucker. When people are around you. You just drain their energy and they're like, "You know what, she's just in a daze," and you want people to enjoy to be around you so your spouse may have a difficult time being around you. If you're complaining a lot or if you are having low energy, kind of boring, not spontaneous, the life or the youthfulness of you has left. Now, I don't want you to feel like I'm beating you up and

I'm not blaming you at all. I want to encourage you to see the power that you have within you to change your situation.

If you want to be happy, make a decision to be:

Happy No Matter What, No Matter What I'm Going To Love Myself, No Matter What I'm Going To Love Myself, No Matter What I'm Going To Love Myself, No Matter What I'm Going To Love Myself. No Matter What I Decide To Love Me So That I Can Love You.

Repeat that as many times as you need to in order for it to get into your spirit so that it's not just words, but you are giving yourself the power and permission to be loved by God and for God to you and show you your worth and your value so that you will never feel unloved another day in your life. You teach people how to treat you and when you fall in love with who God made you to be, other people will see your value and if they don't, that's their fault and not yours, but you make a decision to love yourself and watch other people fall in love with you too.

Lastly, loving yourself will also allow you to notice abuse. It will expose the hurt in others. Have you ever heard the saying, "Hurt people, hurt others?" That means that people who are contributing to hurting others, are often times hurt badly. The only thing that can stop them from their bad habits is love and compassion. When you're able to show compassion, you won't take things so personally. That doesn't mean that you have to endure mistreatment. It means that you can find strength to

49

love someone from a distance until they get the help that they need. We are not God and staying in an abusive relationship will not change that person. Only God can change someone. God's wants you to know how much your loved and wants to remind you of your worth. If you're in an abusive relationship, remember to love yourself. Loving yourself cannot be taken from you. Never allow someone to take your mind. You can always pray for strength silently and God will give you that strength. Loving yourself will afford you to make better decisions out of love and not fear. You're never alone. God is with you and within. Choose you!!!!

PSA: If you feel that your life is being threaten, you should seek help. Sometimes loving someone can put you in danger. If your marriage is putting you in harm's way, find peace in knowing that you did nothing to make someone treat you so badly. That's a choice that they have made and you must ensure your safety at all times. Get help to remove yourself if God as told you to do so. Meditation allow you to hear from God clearly. If you are in doubt rather you should leave or not, seek the guidance of God and do as He instructs. God loves you and will not want you to be abused.

Day 14

Affirmation:

It is My Responsibility to Love Myself.

Prayer:

He that getteth wisdom loveth his own soul: he that keepeth understanding shall find good. Be strong and of a good courage, fear not, nor be afraid of them: for the LORD thy God, he [it is] that doth go with thee; he will not fail thee, nor forsake thee. Love the Lord your God with all your heart and with all your soul and with all your mind and with all your strength. The second is this: 'Love your neighbor as yourself. There is no commandment greater than these." And So, It Is!

Day 15

Affirmation:

I am Loved.

I am Strong.

I like Myself.

I Love Myself.

I will Speak Kindly to Myself.

I will not give Up, I deserve the best and my best life is here to claim today.

I will not self-sabotage my happiness.

I am Great.

I am Beautiful

I Give and receive love easily and unconditionally

I Am Loved by God

I Am Creating the best version of Myself

I Am Worthy

Prayer:

Dear Heavenly Father God I am so grateful to be loved by you. I know that I am never alone. You give me strength on my days of weakness and remind me that I am more than a conqueror. Teach me how to love myself in the way that I think, live, treat others, speak, and give. I am part of you and I am worthy of love. I am loved. And So It Is, Amen.

Day 16

Affirmation:

When days seem difficult, I renew my mind in lovin thoughts.

When my self-esteem is low, I renew my mind with loving thoughts.

When I'm around unloving people, I renew my mind to create the love that I desire.

I have the divine power within me to shift atmospheres.

I have the divine power within me to love the unlovable.

I have the divine power within me to bring Heaven to earth.

I am creating a loving life.

Prayer

Lord allow me to love and receive love. Teach me how to receive love and soften my heart to show compassion towards unloving people. Teach me not to judge others, who are not aware of your love towards them. Give me grace and show me how to extend grace to others. And So, It Is!

Day 17

Affirmation:

I am....

Worthy

Loved

Healthy

Wealthy

Chosen

Free

I am Manifesting My Best Life as It Is in Heaven

Prayer:

Lord remind me of my true identity in you as I mediate on your word. Remove the chatter from my mind that tries to convince me that I am not like you. Give me patience to hear from you and not come up with my own ideas, but wait until you reveal your truth to me. You said in your word to, "seek first the kingdom of God and Your righteous and all things shall be added to me." I believe it and I receive it, And So It Is. Amen

Day 18

Affirmation:

I Choose to Forgive.

Prayer:

"Judge not, and you will not be judged; condemn not, and you will not be condemned; forgive, and you will be forgiven. No temptation has overtaken you that is not common to man. God is faithful, and he will not let you be tempted beyond your ability, but with the temptation he will also provide the way of escape, that you may be able to endure it. Surely there is not a righteous man on earth who does good and never sins. Let all bitterness and wrath and anger and clamor and slander be put away from you, along with all malice. Be kind to one another, tenderhearted, forgiving one another, as God in Christ forgave you. And So, It Is!

05

CHAPTER

05

Teach Him How to Love You

———————— ⚜ ————————

Over the years you may have changed and your husband may not know exactly how to love you anymore. Maybe he feels as if things were one way at one point in time and now things are different and so now it's just kind of chaos or there may be some distance. The reality is we change, change is inevitable and it's going to happen and so do you. And so it's so important to date and to rediscover each other because you're constantly changing and your spouse's constantly changing as well. And so, in this season, you may know what you need or what you desire from your spouse.

But they may not know exactly what it is that you are seeking from them, your expectations may not be no. So what do you do? You teach him how to love you by giving him what you want. If you want your husband to be more loving then I challenge you to love him more. If you want your spouse to be more understanding, then I'm asking you to understand him more. If your example is, I want him to treat me like a queen, my advice to you is to be his queen, I'm sorry. If you want him to treat you like a queen, you need to present him to your household, and you need to treat him and honor him like the king.

It's easy to be a king when you have a queen honoring you. It's easy to love someone when you realize they won't give up on you and they decide that they're going to love you no matter what that have got bay, that unconditional love, give what you want, you know the law of sowing and reaping. What have you sown into your marriage lately? You desire more romance, but you go on a bed with sweat pants on. You want your husband to look at you and desire you and you may want him to appreciate you and look at you and say, "Man, my wife is beautiful." Do you feel like you're beautiful? Because it's not fair to put an expectation on your husband that you don't even see in yourself. You may want your husband to find you to be sexy. Okay, well are you sexy or do you want him to just imagine you to be sexy? So you have to be honest with you on where you're at because see, this is not about him, it's about you. And it's about you just being honest with who you are. And once you become honest about who you are, you can literally change some things in your everyday life to get different results.

Do you want your husband to flirt with you more. Okay, flirt with him more, send him a message that doesn't have anything to do with, "what he want for dinner or that you're going to pick the kids up from practice or something dealing with anything other than pouring into your marriage". Not day to day life, I'm talking about *your marriage*. And when you decide to do that, you're teaching him how to treat you, how to love you.

He may not know but you know what you want, you're a woman, you're not a little girl, you're a woman. So show your man what you like.

Your husband can tell if you don't like him. If you're struggling with this, try to write in a gratitude journal all the things that you like in your husband. The things that you ponder on the most will be magnified and will continue to manifest itself. What are you focused on?

Day 19

Affirmation:

I will say kind things to myself and replace all negative thoughts of myself with the truth and love of God.

I will train myself to see the good in others, especially my husband.

I will become want I want in my marriage.

I will replace all negative thoughts of my husband with the truth and love of God.

I decide to build my marriage up, affirming the word of God over it, instead of tearing it down with resentment, fear, hurt, and dishonor.

Prayer:

Lord strengthen my mind and expand my heart. Keep my mind on you and not of the things of this world that promotes fear. I choose to live in truth. That truth is that I'm loved and I welcome love. I receive love easy and unconditionally. I am created to create. I have the power within me to shift atmospheres and bring love with me wherever I go. And So, It Is!

Day 20

Affirmation:

I support my husband.

I support his visions and his dreams.

I honor his words and truth his heart.

I respect his counsel and honor his position as the head of our family.

I welcome his love and will continue to love him unconditionally.

Prayer:

God thank you for your divine power to love the unlovable. I release my expectations of a perfect man and except my husband as he is. I welcome your guidance and correction in our marriage. Teach us to move as one and to work together as a team. And it is so.

Day 21

Affirmation:

I choose to See Love, Feel Love, and to Show Love.

Prayer:

Kiss me and kiss me again, for your love is sweeter than wine. Love is patient, love is kind. It does not envy, it does not boast, it is not proud. It is not rude, it is not self-seeking, it is not easily angered, it keeps no record of wrongs. Love does not delight in evil but rejoices with the truth. It always protects, always trusts, always hopes, always perseveres. Love never fails. My lover is mine, and I am his. Above all, love each other deeply, because love covers over a multitude of sins. And So, It Is!

Day 22

Affirmation:

I Provide Peace for My home and a place of refuge for my husband.

Prayer:

The wise woman builds her house, but with her own hands the foolish one tears hers down. A soft answer turneth away wrath: but grievous words stir up anger.

The tongue of the wise useth knowledge aright: but the mouth of fools poureth out foolishness. A wholesome tongue is a tree of life: but perverseness therein is a breach in the spirit. And So, It Is!

06

CHAPTER

06

Create a New Story

What story have you created in your mind and in your spirit about your marriage? This is very important because when we create a story in our minds, in our hearts, in our spirits, then life has to produce different circumstances in order to support our story because we don't want to tell ourselves that our stories untrue. So if you have decided in your mind, your heart and your spirit that you have unloving husband, then you're going to manifest certain situations and circumstances that validate how you feel and the story that you have told yourself. Now keep in mind, it's all about perception and energy. And so once you decide who your husband is to you, he's going to do things and say things that validate how you feel to make your story true and real to you. How could this be the case? You may ask, well your husband to you may be unloving, but someone else that you know very closely, maybe not his mother or another relative may view him very differently than you view him.

And that's because they have a different experience with him and they have a different story of him or whatever the case is. So are you willing to rewrite your story? Now, this is some work. Let me tell you, are you willing to rewrite your story in what you told yourself about your marriage and about your husband? If you are, then I congratulate you because it's going to take courage to tell yourself, "Okay, I'm done reading that book, I'm ready for the next chapter, I'm ready to see my husband in a different life." And so in order to do this, I need you two view your husband only in the way that you want your new story to read. So if you tell yourself, I want to thank God for my loving husband, once you start telling yourself that story enough, you'll start believing the story. And once you start believing the story, you adapt a new belief system regarding your husband and then things, circumstances and situations will then start to change and occurred to support your new story. He will do things that are more loving, he will say things that are more appreciative, your story will change once you decide to change how you view him. Now I know you probably thinking I'm crazy and that's fine, but I will tell you that this is the true. God gave you the power to create and I'm going to share a secret with you. I was never really a person who did affirmations or manifestation exercises until about maybe six years ago. I started doing little things because I found myself becoming negative Nancy, just with everything.

I was the type of person that was just skeptical about anybody, I didn't really see the good in them. I thought everybody was coming at an angle, I was very protective and defensive because I felt like made me that way. And then I chose to be more loving and see the world from a different lens. And that happened once I change the story in my head and said, "The world is not all terrible, there is the loving people and loving experiences," and God changed my perspective on the world. Now, I see it as a beautiful place. Yes, the bad things and terrible things happen but it's still a beautiful place to live and loving other people. It's just an amazing feeling and relationships and community and I can go on and on and on. But you're going to see what you decide to see, if you want to see all the crime and all the chaos in the world, and that's what you focus on. That's what you'll see through your lens, but if you want to see the world through another lens, through a Godly view then you also see the love that's also here as well.

And so as you begin to tell yourself another story, it's going to feel like you're telling yourself a lie, it's going to feel like you are just blatantly lie, lying, lying, lying to yourself. That's what it's going to feel like. But then you have to remember the power of your words and that you have power to create. So I would say not three years ago I started a manifestation box and they were really my prayers, and whatever I wanted to see God change in my life I would write the opposite of what was going on. And this is not just regarding my marriage, this is regarding every area of my life. And I remember doing this with my weight, I felt like after having five children, I felt like my body was changing and I can't really lose the weight that I wanted and it was just really frustrating. And so I would write a lie on my little notebook paper, "Lord, I thank you for being loving and kind to me and allowing me to have a healthy, happy life. And I thank you for allowing me to be a healthy way. And I love the way that I look, I feel good in my clothes. I have awesome self-esteem." I would write everything that was the opposite of how I felt that day. Whatever I felt that particular moment, I would write a letter to God, the opposite of what it was. And I would thank him and it's just so amazing because then I will look through my manifestation box months or even years later and I would see all these things that I wrote that came to past and that was my present moment reality And I remember thinking to myself like, "This is so amazing because I know for a fact that when I wrote this statement on this paper, that was not the case because it's in my manifestation box, which means I was speaking in distance because it did not exist at that moment in my life." So if you don't believe me, that's fine, I'm just encouraging you to just try it. What do you have to lose? You're not happy right now anyway.

So why not say to yourself, "I am not going to say another negative thing about my spouse to me, to a family member, to a friend, to no one. I will only speak highly of my husband. I will only give my husband the love and respect that he is deserving of, I will only honor my husband in a respectful way. I mean, whatever it is, just declare it, just declare it and tell yourself that I am rewriting my marital story right now. And so it is in Jesus' name and I counted as done and Lord, I thank you. Rewrite your story today. What do you want to write today that doesn't exist? And once you start to close your eyes and imagine your new story playing out in your life and you're smiling and you could feel the energy and the love in your home and you can feel the love and compassion and understanding and all those feelings that make you feel good about your marriage, you feel those coming back. And just take about five minutes during the day and just start to see it in your mind.

Because if you can see it, it will manifest. So if you're having a hard time changing things in your life, chances are it's because you can't see it. And if you can't see it, it's not going to manifest. Nobody builds them all, they can't see. They see the blueprint in their head first, they see how they want this mall to be and then they can take that vision and make a blueprint, and from the blueprint they build it and then there you go. You have a mall that you're shopping in.

And so I encourage you to sit in silence until you can see it, imagine it, if you can't see it, imagine it and imagine it until you can't see it. And tell yourself a new story, write a new story for your marriage, and watch a new marriage manifest. So get a little cute box or get a shoe box or get something where you can write little letters to God manifesting right in it as if it already is. Folded up and then look back on it later and it's just amazing when you see these miracles in your life and you open up your manifestation box and all those things have come to past, it's a great feeling. So rewrite your story today, you have the power to do it. God gave you power to create. So create a new story.

Day 23

Affirmation:

I write my own "Love Story", and it is beautiful. I have the power to create and not destroy.

Prayer:

Death and life are in the power of the tongue, and those who love it will eat its fruits. So shall my word be that goes out from my mouth; it shall not return to me empty, but it shall accomplish that which I purpose, and shall succeed in the thing for which I sent it. Truly, I say to you, whoever says to this mountain, 'Be taken up and thrown into the sea,' and does not doubt in his heart, but believes that what he says will come to pass, it will be done for him. Since we have the same spirit of faith according to what has been written, "I believed, and so I spoke," we also believe, and so we also speak. And whatever you ask in prayer, you will receive, if you have faith." I speak life over my marriage and cover it with the blood of Jesus, And So It Is, Amen.

Day 24

Affirmation:

I Am Ready for My Happiness. I receive and welcome it. I give myself permission to love and to recognize love. I have the strength to remove toxic people from my life and the wisdom to know who those people are. I AM loved by God and seek Him for my divine direction. I will not speak badly about my husband as we are one flesh, but commit to love, honor, and respect him as my covering.

Prayer:

Wives, submit to your own husbands, as to the Lord. An excellent wife who can find? She is far more precious than jewels. The heart of her husband trusts in her, and he will have no lack of gain. She does him good, and not harm, all the days of her life. But I want you to understand that the head of every man is Christ, the head of a wife is her husband, and the head of Christ is God. And so, train the young women to love their husbands and children, to be self-controlled, pure, working at home, kind, and submissive to their own husbands, that the word of God may not be reviled. An excellent wife is the crown of her husband, but she who shames him is as rottenness in his bones." And So, It Is!

Day 25

Affirmation:

I will please my husband and honor him in all ways.

Prayer:

Let him kiss me with the kisses of his mouth for your love is more delightful than wine. My beloved is to me a sachet of myrrh resting between my breasts. How right they are to adore you! Oh, how charming! And our bed is verdant. My beloved is mine and I am his. Let my beloved come into his garden and taste its choice fruits. And So, It Is!

Day 26

Affirmation:

I will bring honor to my husband and to my home.

Prayer:

For wisdom is better than jewels, and all that you may desire cannot compare with her. The heart of her husband trusts in her, and he will have no lack of gain. He who finds a wife finds a good thing and obtains favor from the LORD. And though your beginning was small, your latter days will be very great. And So, It Is!

07

CHAPTER

07

Perception Versus Deception

———— ❧ ————

The enemy loves to deceive us and to get us to pay attention to things that don't really exist. And like the chapter about your story, you will start to paint pictures in your head and you will begin to see things that aren't there sometimes. And it's not to discredit any situation or anything like that, but there are perceptions that you may have but depending on what angle you decide to look at, you can also be deceived as well. This is very important because you just want to make sure that you're always praying and asking God to show you true. The enemy will come and give you suggestions. And also will accuse because he's the accuser. And so a lot of times the things that are brought to us are not the true, the enemy will give you lies. And so a lie could be something as simple as but as hurtful as, you see, your husband walked in the door and he didn't even speak to you. He doesn't love you. Okay, let's pause.

So, your husband comes in and not speak to you, you may not realize why or whatever the case is, but the enemy instantly tells you that he doesn't love you. It's not like your husband walked in the door and said, "I don't love you." But the enemy will say he doesn't love you and your husband can be feeling like, "I love my family. That's why I'm out here working every day. I walked through the door and I'm tired, but I hope my wife realized how much I love her."

So with that example right there, we're dealing with perception versus deception. Your husband is perceiving that you know how much you're love because he just walked in the door and he's tired because he didn't work the double shift or whatever the case is. But the enemy try to deceive you by saying, "He don't love you." He walked in and he was speed.

And so well, we start to live in a lie in deception, we're really so deceived that we can self-sabotage our own marriage just based off of who you're listening to and who you're believing. Are you standing on the word of God? Are you speaking to those mountains that are coming and that are posing challenges in your marriage? Or are you just laying down and being deceived and you're taking whatever lie that Satan gives you? You have to get to the point in your faith where you make a decision, who are you going to trust and who are you going to believe? Now, I know that may be difficult for some people depending on where you are and your level of faith, but I will tell you this, Satan is the father of lies and so whatever he's telling you, the truth is the opposite of that. There are times when husbands can get frustrated and depending on what tools they're working with, they don't know how to always navigate those frustrations and so it comes on in different ways. I don't want you guys to think that I'm making any excuses for any behavior that a husband is showing, unloving ways towards his wife or anything like that. But what I am saying is, if your husband is lacking or not utilizing his tools correctly, why would you expect anything less? If your husband is not spending time with God, why did you expect him to be this man of wisdom and he should know certain things where he's not being guided on how to even love you or be a great husband if he's not in the presence of God.

There are certain things that he just may not be displayed because he's weak in that area. And whenever your spirit is weak, your fleshes always want to override, and it's the same true for us. If you are starving your spirit and you're feeding your flesh, whatever stronger, it's what's going to show up in your life. I remember a young lady very frustrated, and she told me her husband was cheating on her and she had all these expectations really of a godly man, but her husband, he wasn't spending time with the Lord, even half of his spirit strong enough to behave any differently.

And so after working with her, she decided maybe my expectations are unrealistic, I'm expecting godly results from a worldly man. And that's what happens. Why do you expect someone to be faithful to you if they're feeding into their flesh and their spirit is weak, that's what happens. And so you have to ask yourself, what expectations do you have? If you want someone to grow closer to the Lord, then that's something you will put in your manifestation, something you want to speak into existence. Lord, I thank you for allowing my husband to create time with you for guidance, counsel, for love, direction, for our family, and to help with his daily life. Lord, I thank you for teaching him how to love me. Whatever the case is, write it down and create your new story, but always keep in mind what's your perception of your husband versus the deception. How are you viewing your husband and from what lens? Is it from a lens of, is it unloving? Because if you're viewing him in unloving way, then that's not of God either. So sit down with yourself and ask yourself, "Are you truly seeing him as God would have you see your marriage?"

I understand that he may actually be an unloving person, however, some point in time you saw enough love in him to marry him. Perhaps he changed with time, resentment could have taken him hostage, and he could feel lost in life in general. A lost man will eventually lose confidence in himself and his ability to be a great husband. It could also affect his performance at work.

Regardless, you choose your husband and you made vows to stay for better or worse. Unless your life is threatened physically or mentally, you should ask consider that it may just be a season. I never tell wives to leave or stay in their marriage. Truth is, you only answer to God and God alone. No one is walking in your shoes every day. So please do not feel like this book is beating you up. My goal is to off you a different perspective. You are not a victim, that would make you helpless. You are not weak nor helpless. You have the power of the Holy Spirit flowing throw you. You choose that man and that marriage. And you can now choose to love and honor your husband even at the times when he is being unloving. Have you ever acted unloving towards him? Of course not! Yeah right, we all have.

There was a time when a wife reached out to me and said, "I just don't feel the love anymore," I replied, "What's love got to do with it?" See, people fall in and out of love depending on their psyche. Love is a choice, you commit to loving your husband. You don't just say, "I DO", at the altar, you say it every day. God gives you want you need, not always what you want? Often times it's the storms that build our character.

Believe or not, a lot of husbands and wives are guilty of idolizing each other. The Word of God reminds us not to have any other God before Him. Therefor be careful of wanting your husband to idolize you. It's seen in marriages so often and God is not pleased. I know, the idea of your husband worshipping the ground that you walk on seems to be appealing, however, as wives your spirit does not want to b worshipped, your ego does. There is no room for ego in a marriage. Once ego enters the picture, here comes chaos to follow shortly behind it. The ego cannot be pleased and you'll get tried trying to make ego happy. Who is desiring more love, your true self or your ego?

Love is a beautiful thing. God is love and choosing to love no matter what is choosing God. I have this saying, if you want to get closer to God, Get Married." That statement is so true. Choosing to love is choosing to commit.

Day 27

Affirmation:

I will acknowledge that Love is always the answer to any problem that I may have in my marriage.

Prayer:

Lord teach me to love more.

Day 28

Affirmation:

My husband and I are on the same team and I speak unity over my marriage.

Prayer:

"Therefore, a man shall leave his father and his mother and hold fast to his wife, and they shall become one flesh." Therefore, what God has joined together, let no one separate. And So, it Is!

Day 29

Affirmation:

I will let go of anything, anyone, including thoughts that are not promoting a healthy marriage and mindset. I will honor my mental space and control my negative thoughts.

Prayer:

Do not conform to the pattern of this world, but be transformed by the renewing of your mind. Then you will be able to test and approve what God's will is—his good, pleasing and perfect will.

Day 30

Affirmation:

I Am committed to being the best version of myself. I will see my life and my marriage through a spiritual lens and trust God for everything. I have the power within me to overcome any obstacle within my marriage. I will count my blessings. I believe in my marriage.

CHAPTER

Prayer

———— ✦ ————

Staying connected is so important to everyone. In the household. Your children will thank you, your marriage will thank you, your co-workers will thank you and his co-workers will thank you. Everybody's going to thank you when you guys are staying connected and keeping a smile on each other's face. Point blank period. If there is sexual frustration in your marriage, it's going to show out. Your husband maybe walking around, mad, with attitude, you're like, "I don't know what's wrong with him. He's not very loving. He's not very nice. He's not very affectionate." Ask yourself, when was the last time you connect it with your husband without him initiating it? Now, we're all grownups, so when I say connected with your husband, I mean when was the last time you and your husband made love? When's the last time y'all had sex? Just in the middle of the day and it wasn't planned and it's just very spontaneous because a man needs to know that his wife is desiring him. Man, do not like rejection, just like a woman does not like rejection. When you are having sex with your spouse and he feels like you're doing it as a chore, that puts him in a mood of, "Is she really desiring me?" My husband and I wrote a book years ago, it was called, Not Tonight, I'm Tired." We wrote that book to help encourage couples stay connected, it was a fun way, it was like a little game in there that we mentioned. It's a fun way to keep couples connected, but at the end of the day, women know when your husband aiming getting in. And I know this is the last thing you want to hear right now, because you're feeling unloved and you may not feel secure in your marriage or whatever the case is, but I'm telling you this out of love, because if your husband is going places and he sexually frustrated, people can sense that and it's hurtful not only to him, but it's hurtful to you because you don't want your husband walking around looking vulnerable to other women.

Because if you're not initiating in his ear and flirting with him, then that leaves room for the enemy to come in. Affairs don't start in the bed, they start in conversations. If your husband is not feeling desired by you, more than likely he may not open up to you as much and he may not share as much about his day or what's going on with him, he may start to be a little bit more reserve, where you guys are not having those intimate conversations anymore. So this advice in this chapter is to be his piece, to be his peace of mind, knowing that he's secure with you, that he can give his heart and his body to you and that you're going to love and honor him and respect him as the head of the house, as your husband. A man needs to feel like he's the king of something if he doesn't feel like he's the king at your house, you don't want him going searching for a kingdom because he feels like he has none. Be his piece, his piece, his piece of bullying, his piece of late night loving, his piece, piece, P-I-E-C-E, his piece. Be his piece so he won't need no side piece. Now, I know everybody is married to a man of God. Hallelujah! But your man is still a whole man. He's still a man and he's still living in this flesh with all this temptation around here, we're big booty Judy down the street, and all these desperate women out here that's just waiting to break up a happy home. And is your home happy? Because that's what you would blame it on the other woman saying she broke up your happy home. Well, I mean, can she? Can someone do that? I don't know. I'm just speculating right now, I'm not trying to step on nobody's toes, I'm trying to help you out of love, get out of the space of being unloved because you are loved, you're a child of God to raise your vibration to a higher standard of a calling of being a wife and being the best wife that you can be. So that your husband feels loved and secure to be yourself and why is he frustrated with life.

Everything has a route. So if your husband is being unloving towards you or resentful or whatever the case is, I asked you to take me for the Lord in prayer to find the roots and to speak to the roots and speak love and life to the root of the issue so that you and your husband can get the healing that you need so that you can move forward with a happy and prosperous life together.

I believe in the power of God, so if you're waiting for your husband to make some changes before your marriage gets better, I would suggest that you trust God. Through God, he can get the strength to do X, Y, Z, or through God you can get the strength to make changes and do X, Y, Z. But what I do know, without God and you're trying to do it, and he trying to do it, it's going to be very difficult. It's going to be very difficult whenever you exclude God from your marriage. But whenever you ask God, when you look within and you ask the Holy Spirit within you to guide you in how you speak, how you act, how you carry yourself, you allow God to change. Stop trying to be the holy spirit in your husband's life, you can't change him, nor should you want to. You shouldn't want to control people, you shouldn't want to change people, but God will allow us to have power and influence with those who love us, who want to change. So I'm going to leave you with this. If you haven't learned anything in this book, I hope that you have learned how precious you are to God. And once you change the way you see yourself, you will encourage and inspire other people to look at you differently. They're like something about her. She got a glow all of a sudden. When you start feeling good about yourself, other people will notice. I don't feel like you can never go wrong whenever you invest in your relationship with God and whenever you invest in bettering yourself as a woman. You can never lose, you can never lose when you discover the true identity that God has created you to be, you will always win, you will always be on top knowing who you are in Christ Jesus and you're walking confidently.

Love your king, so that he can crown you as queen, but you can't walk around the house as queen and you're dishonoring your king. Now, I don't know everybody's individual situations but I hope that there is a chapter in this book to at least speak to the area of your life in order for you to get help some people may need some counsel and go to a couple, or someone who loves the couple. I don't think it's wise to ever talk about your marriage with your single friends. Never, ever, ever, never, ever, I don't care how wise they are, if they're single, it's just wise to, they're speaking from a certain level. And I really believe that it's important to get help before it's too late, before the heart has grown hard. And so, my prayer is that any marriage that the heart remains soft and even if it's hard, God has a way of making the hard tender again. You're not unloved, I know the book got your attention because that's how you're feeling right now but I want to encourage you and I want to tell you, and I want to remind you that you're beautiful. That you're deserving of a great marriage, that you're loved, that you're an exceptional woman, that you're beautiful inside and out. And that you have so much to give to yourself, allow yourself to be loved by you and allow yourself to be loved by others. When people give you a compliment, say thank you, don't doubt it, just receive. Sometimes we're good givers but we're not very good receivers. So I pray that you're a great receiver in this season of your life as well. Receive the love from God, receive the love from yourself and receive the love from your husband. And so it is in Jesus' name. Amen.

Sometimes wives feel unloved but may not understand why.

30-Day Praying for Your Husband Challenge

"She does him good . . ." (Proverbs 31:12a)

Day 1

Pray that your husband will grow spiritually and consider his accountability before the Lord. Pray that he will guard his heart by developing spiritual disciplines—Bible reading and study, prayer, meditation, scripture memorization, etc. (2 Peter 3:18; Prov. 4:23)

Day 2

Pray that your husband's relationship with God and His Word will bear fruit in his life. Pray that he will be a man of wisdom and understanding, fearing the Lord. (Prov. 3:7, 9:10; Ps. 112:1)

Day 3

Pray that your husband will be humble and quick to agree with God about his sin. Pray that his heart will be tender toward the voice of the Lord. (Ps. 51:2-4; Micah 6:8)

Day 4

Pray that your husband will grow in leadership skills in your relationship—protecting and providing for you. Pray that he will lead you wisely and love you sacrificially, so that God will be glorified in your marriage. (Eph. 5:25-29; Col. 3:19)

Day 5

Pray that your husband will be faithful to his wedding vows. Pray that he will have a desire to cultivate your relationship as a sign of his loyalty and commitment to you, and as a picture of Christ's love for the Church. (Prov. 20:6; Gen. 2:24)

Day 6

Pray that your husband will love righteousness and hate wickedness, especially the evils of the culture. Pray that he will recognize and avoid wickedness in his own life, and if necessary, take a clear, strong stand against evil. (Prov. 27:12; John 17:15; 1 Cor. 10:12-13)

Day 7

Pray that your husband will safeguard his heart against inappropriate relationships with the opposite sex. Pray that his heart will be pure and undivided in his commitment to you. (Prov. 6:23-24, 26; Rom. 13:14)

Day 8

Pray that your husband will work hard to provide for your family, to the best of his ability. Pray that the character qualities necessary for a successful career and ministry will be a growing part of his character—persistence, decisiveness, strength, an analytical mind, organizational skills, positive relationships with people, determination, etc. (Rom. 12:11; 1 Cor. 15:58)

Day 9

Pray that your husband handle finances wisely, will have discernment concerning budgeting and investments, and will be a good steward of his money in regard to giving to the Lord's work. *Pray that money will not become a source of discord in your family. (Prov. 23:4-5; Rom. 12:13; Heb. 13:5)*

Day 10

Pray that your husband will cultivate strong integrity, and not compromise his convictions. Pray that his testimony will be genuine, that he will be honest in his business dealings, and will never do anything that he needs to hide from others. (Prov. 20:7; 1 Tim. 1:5, 3:7; Eph. 6:10-12)

Day 11

Pray that your husband will have a humble, teachable spirit and a servant's heart before the Lord. Pray that he will listen to God and desire to do His will. (Prov. 15:33; Eph. 6:6)

Day 12

Pray that your husband will yield his sexual drive to the Lord and practice self-control. Pray that your sexual intimacy together will be fresh, positive, and a reflection of selfless love. (Prov. 5:15, 18; 1 Cor. 7:3; Song of Solomon 7:10)

Day 13

Pray that your husband uses practical skills to build your family and make wise decisions for your welfare. Pray that he will serve unselfishly. (Gal. 5:13; Phil. 2:3-4)

Day 14

Pray that your husband will speak words that build you and your family, and reflect a heart of love. Pray that he will not use filthy language. (Prov. 18:21; Eph. 4:29)

Day 15

Pray that your husband will choose his friends wisely. Pray that God will bring him men who will encourage his accountability before God, and will not lead him into sin. (Prov. 13:20; Prov. 27:17)

Day 16

Pray that your husband will choose healthy, God-honoring activities. Pray that he will not live in bondage to any questionable habits or hobbies, but that he will experience freedom in holiness as he yields to the Spirit's control. (1 Cor. 6:12, 10:31; 2 Tim. 2:4)

Day 17

Pray that your husband will enjoy his manliness as he patterns his life after Christ and strong men in the faith. Pray for his physical, emotional, mental, social and spiritual strength. (Eph. 3:16; 1 Peter 2:21; 1 Cor. 10:11)

Day 18

Pray that your husband will have an eternal perspective—living in light of eternity. Pray that he will reject materialism and temporal values and put God first in his life. *(Matt. 6:33; Deut. 6:5; Eph. 5:16; Ps. 90:12)*

Day 19

Pray that your husband will be patient and a man of peace. Pray that he will not give in to anger, but will allow the Holy Spirit to control his responses. *(Rom. 14:19; Ps. 34:14)*

Day 20

Pray that your husband will yield his mind and thoughts to the Lord. Pray that he will not entertain immoral or impure thoughts, and that he will resist the temptation to indulge in pornography. *(Prov. 27:12; 2 Cor. 10:5)*

Day 21

Pray that your husband will learn how to relax in the Lord and, in his greatest times of stress, find joy and peace in his relationship with God. Pray that he will submit his schedule to the Lord. *(Neh. 8:10; Prov. 17:22; Ps. 16:11)*

Day 22

Pray that your husband will practice forgiveness in your relationship and with others. Pray that he will recognize any roots of bitterness, and yield any resentment and unforgiving attitudes to the Lord. *(Eph. 4:32; Heb. 12:15)*

Day 23

Pray that your husband will be a good father—disciplining his children wisely and loving them unconditionally. If he is not a *father, pray that he will find a young man to mentor in the things of the Lord. (Eph. 6:4; Col. 3:21; 2 Tim. 2:1-2)*

Day 24

Pray that your husband will have a balanced life—that he will balance work and play. Pray that he will fear God, but also gain favor with people he knows at work and church. (Luke 2:52; Prov. 13:15)

Day 25

Pray that your husband will be courageous in his stand against evil and injustice, and that he will stand for the truth. Pray that he will protect you and your family from Satan's attacks. (Ps. 31:24; Eph. 6:13; Ps. 27:14)

Day 26

Pray that your husband will discover and live his God-given purpose. Pray that he will offer all his dreams to the Lord, and pursue only those goals that will bring God glory and count for eternity. (Jer. 29:11; 1 Cor. 10:31)

Day 27

Pray that your husband will understand the importance of taking care of his body—the temple of the Holy Spirit—for the glory of God. Pray that he will practice self-control by making wise food choices, and get sufficient exercise to stay healthy. (Rom. 12:1-2; 1 Cor. 6:19-20, 9:27)

Day 28

Pray that your husband will be a man of prayer. Pray that he will seek and pursue God in purposeful quiet times. (1 Thess. 5:17; Luke 22:46; James 5:16)

Day 29

Pray that your husband will surrender his time and talents to the Lord. Pray that his spiritual gifts will be manifest in his career, at church, and in your home. (Eph. 5:15-16; 1 Cor. 12:4, 7)

Day 30

Pray that your husband will serve God and others with pure motives. Pray that he will obey the Lord from his heart, and glorify Him in everything. (1 Cor. 10:13; John 7:17-18; Col. 3:23-24)

About Author

Dr. Marita has inspired thousands of people to overcome adversity with triumph through faith and perseverance. While facing several life-changing challenges herself, Marita had enough faith to conquer tribulations, coming out victorious. With over 12 years of experience in life coaching, writing, and helping people to heal their soul, she captures the true essence of what it means to turn "lemons into lemonade", she has taken the harsh lessons of life and developed a plan for successful living.

She is best known for her heartfelt inspirational books. Dr. Kinney's writing has afforded her the opportunity to travel all over the country spreading the wonderful joys of her faith. That's where her journey began as a Life Coach. Supporters from across the country began seeking Mrs. Kinney's inspiration and encouragement.

Marita then furthered her education and obtained her certification for Life Coaching through The Life Purpose Institute and became Board Certified through The Center for Credentialing and Education (C.C.E), as an affiliate of the National Board for Certified Counselors. She is an ordinated minister and holds her Doctorate degree in Metaphysical Science from the University of Sedona. She has authored over 58 books and has helped thousands of people move from a broken dark place in life to a meaningful life, with purpose, and joy.

Dr. Kinney's coaching skills allow her clients to easily obtain the necessary steps to move forward. She has been featured on The Steve Harvey Show, Business magazines, and countless interviews. She is married to Rev. Dr. Demoine Kinney and they have six children.

Specialty: Holistic Counseling for Trauma, Grief/Loss, Marriage, Therapeutic Writing and Career.

www.maritakinney.com

www.purethoughtspublishing.com

Notes

Notes

Notes

Notes

Notes

Notes

Notes

Notes

Notes

Notes

Notes

Notes

Notes

Notes

Notes

Notes

Notes

Notes

Notes

Notes

Notes

Notes

Notes

Notes

Notes

Notes

Notes

Notes

Notes

Notes

Notes

Notes

Notes

Notes

Notes

Notes

Notes

Notes

Notes

Notes

Notes

Notes

Notes

Notes

Notes

Notes

Notes

Notes

Notes

Notes

Notes

Notes

Notes

Notes

Notes

Notes

Notes

Notes

Notes

Notes

Notes

Notes

Notes

Notes

Notes

Notes

Notes

Notes

Notes

Notes

www.ingramcontent.com/pod-product-compliance
Lightning Source LLC
Chambersburg PA
CBHW032352280326
41935CB00008B/548